ALCATRAZ

ALCATRAZ
The Rock

Photographs by Ed Beyeler
Foreword by Wallace Stegner
Essay by Susan Lamb

NORTHLAND PRESS FLAGSTAFF, ARIZONA

Frontispiece: Rain over Alcatraz.

FIRST EDITION
ISBN 0-87358-455-4 hardcover
ISBN 0-87358-456-2 softcover
Library of Congress Catalog Card Number 87-42820
Printed and bound in the United States of America

To Ed Pilley;
whose never-ending help,
energy, and love
brought this book
into existence.

FOREWORD

Wallace Stegner

BLEAK BETWEEN ITS COLD TIDES, swept by sun and fog, waterless, nearly treeless, swarmed over by seabirds, it was one of the first places seen and named by Don Juan Manuel de Ayala when he felt his way into uncharted San Francisco Bay in August, 1775. To different generations it has suggested various uses. For a while during the Spanish-American War it was even used as a rest and recreation area for soldiers suffering from dysentery and other tropical complaints. In recent years, promoters have suggested making it into a water-based resort. From 1969 to 1971 it was occupied by activist Indians and held as a hostage against native treaty claims.

But it was never meant to be a resort or a Pan-Indian school or the headquarters of anything. Certainly it was never created to be a health spa. It feels and has always felt like a fortress or prison. It was the site of the first lighthouse and the first American military installation on the Pacific Coast. During the Civil War it guarded San Francisco Bay without ever having to fire a shot at anyone, and before the war was over it had found its true vocation as a prison from which escape was next to impossible.

Even the soldiers who garrisoned it until the War Department relinquished it in 1934 must have felt like prisoners. How much more passionately, then, must actual prisoners have looked from the fortress rock toward the shores of freedom! First they were Civil War prisoners, then rebellious Indians from Arizona, then deserters from the army in the Philippines, then the inmates of San Francisco's jails, jarred loose by the earthquake and herded out to the island for safekeeping. During World War I the rock held prisoners of war, after the war a variety of military prisoners; and finally, between 1934 and 1962, hard-core public enemies, incorrigibles from every federal prison, were collected on this island of rock and iron under the harshest conditions of maximum security. They were not brought here to be rehabilitated. They were brought to be kept caged like dangerous animals.

What they saw is what Ed Beyeler's camera sees in this book. This lens does not know the color of the sky. Its eye "glances level," and what it knows is the color of steel and stone. Though it is photographing ruins, the ruins are every bit as ominous as the intact structures ever were. These photographs say restriction, lightlessness, damp, limitation, restraint, boredom, despair. It is striking that in all these pages there are only the most fleeting outward looks, mere glimpses caught between lockstep footfalls under the shadow of a gun tower: the Golden Gate Bridge soaring out where seabirds freely go, the City shining on its shore as desirable and unattainable as heaven.

What Ed Beyeler has created is not a documentary study of Alcatraz, certainly not a pictorial history. His book is a longitudinal section of prisoner despair, hopelessness made visible. Its images are of bars, chains, walls, meshes, meager apertures through which leaks a little cold light. If one were to give it a sound track, only one sound would be needed: the clash of steel doors closing, at the touch of an electric key, all down a long, echoing corridor.

PHOTOGRAPHER'S NOTE

Ed Beyeler

On New Year's Day, 1974, I visited "the Rock" for the first time. It was a clear, breezy winter morning, and I took the first ferry out, accompanied by National Park Service personnel. The trip was the result of a request by the park service to record a variety of sites in the newly created Golden Gate National Recreation Area. This was during the period after the Native American occupation but before the government began its restoration effort or opened the island to the public. I anticipated spending not more than a day on the island and, as the day wore on and the aura of the place increasingly depressed me, vowed that I would never return.

I miscalculated. Over a period of two years, I went back to the island more than forty times because I found that, once the initial feeling of gloom wore off, I was intrigued and fascinated by the place; even without a single human inhabitant, it was vital and alive.

Using a 35mm Nikon, 2¼″ Hasselblad, and a 4″ × 5″ view camera and working exclusively with existing light, I spent my time trying to capture the almost-ineffable spirit of this cold place. It was a challenge to translate and convey my emotional response through the lens of my cameras and though the developing and printing of the resulting work.

I hope these photographs convey some of the tremendous impact of Alcatraz as I experienced it, and give the reader another way in which to understand the Rock as it was during a brief moment of its long history.

There is surely a daimon *that dwells in places . . .*
It moves through its people like a vengeful ghost, giving them their dreams.

VINCENT SCULLY

ALCATRAZ
The Rock

Susan Lamb

THE ISLAND OF ALCATRAZ IS HAUNTED by the black dreams of society. The sea mist that shrouds the island in a briny fog also shuts out most of the warmth and light and rusts the iron skeleton of its buildings' concrete walls. Before the National Park Service began to restore and maintain the island's man-made landmarks, years of neglect added to its mystery. Alcatraz has always been a forbidding place, within sight but out of reach, its dismal foghorn a counterpoint to the beauty of the Golden Gate.

Visible from any vantage point on the bay's shore, it has simultaneously repelled and intrigued us for over a century. Most of all, it raises questions. Can a place have such a thing as its own character? Was it always there, or have we burdened it with the worst of man's failings? These twenty-two acres of rocky island, cluttered with broken buildings, a huge water tower, a lighthouse, and crumbling walls, have been the repository for many of society's misfits, and seem to have absorbed their aura.

THE ISLAND, itself an alien presence in San Francisco Bay, is part of a patchwork of terranes, landforms that have a geologic history distinct from that of their neighbors. Alcatraz lies within the embrace of the Golden Gate, but was formed differently than Point Lobos, the Marin Headlands, or Angel Island. Chunks of ocean floor and continent that seem to have no connection to one another were brought into juxtaposition by the forces of plate tectonics, subduction and movement along faultlines. This geologic supposition is supported by the island's marine fossils, which reveal that its rock was formed over one hundred thirty million years ago from a part of the sea floor that must have been near a continent, as turbid currents mixed in sediment of terrestrial origin—quartz, limestone, and shale. For millennia, the terrane drifted in the "slow waltz of the continents" to its present position.

Twenty thousand years ago, sea level was several hundred feet lower than it is today, and the Farallons were not islands but coastline. Alcatraz was a low mountain lying far inland in a valley that had been formed by the erosion of faultlines and two great rivers, the Sacramento and the San Joaquin, which flowed through the Golden Gate to the sea. At the end of the last ice age, the waters of the sea rose and filled the valley. Blue Pacific tides flowed in and out and joined the muddy green river water from California's interior, and Alcatraz was nearly submerged; only its very pinnacle rose above the swirl of water.

To man, Alcatraz has always been an anomaly in the beauty of the bay, an ominous monolith barren except for swarms of shrieking birds. There is little on the island to support human life: no source of fresh water, no naturally occurring edible plants, no convenient nooks or materials for shelter or fuel for fire. Where the waves crash and spray, water creatures cling to the stone, feeding and reproducing to the rhythms of the tides. These barnacles, snails, mussels, and crabs exist on a narrow margin of algaed stone, and seaweed waves eerily at high tide.

The island is a sanctuary for thousands of birds, however, which at first glance seem to be indistinguishable in their numbers and clamor. Careful observation separates the flapping hordes into distinct, individual species; several types of gulls winter here, but it is primarily the western gulls who stay year-round, raising their downy chicks on the steep cliffs. The terns' delicate, pointed wings and forked tails distinguish them from the gulls, while the brown pelicans, who dive into the sea in a jumble of wings and feet, are easily identifiable by their huge, baggy bills. Black oystercatchers with bright orange bills stalk the intertidal zone, and among the dark waterfowl, pelagic cormorants pose at the water's edge, languidly drying their outstretched wings. They are larger than the common murres and coots swimming nearby, or the western grebes, who flash their white throats as they bob on the waves.

FOR CENTURIES, the illusion cast by Alcatraz protected the Golden Gate. Centered behind the mouth of the bay, the island concealed the narrow break in the misty coastline from those who sailed along the coast, seeking safe passage and treasure. Some of the most vigorous seafaring activity occurred during the sixteenth century, when Spanish conquistadores prowled the coast of California in complete ignorance of the enormous bay in which the island lies or of the rich lodes of gold upriver from it; England's Sir Francis Drake, who sailed after them and stole away the wealth of the Spanish armada, may also have sailed obliviously past the Golden Gate. As they gazed landward, it must have appeared to those sailors that the low range of coastal mountains was continuous.

The island's isolation was ended in 1769, however, when a party of Spanish soldiers led by Captain Gaspar de Portolá, travelling overland from Mexico, sighted the natural harbor. Guided by this report, the frigate *San Carlos* sailed into San Francisco Bay in 1775. This tentative probing of the northern California coastline was followed by an onrush of Spaniards, who sought both gold and souls. Although they did not occupy the rocky island, they did give it a name—*alcatraz* comes from the word for a Spanish waterfowl similar to the island's pelicans and cormorants. When Mexico inherited California from Spain in 1822, the fogbound island continued to be ignored.

It was the Americans who first found a use for Alcatraz. In 1846, the United States Army seized California; in the course of inventorying their new territory, they surveyed the island in anticipation of placing fortifications on it to help them maintain their hold on the bay. In their quest to fulfill America's "Manifest Destiny"—expressed in 1845 as being the God-given right to "overspread the continent allotted by Providence for the free development of our multiplying millions"—America's military planners were determined to fend off rival powers hovering nearby. England's powerful fleet was based on Vancouver Island to the north, and Russia, who in 1812 had established Fort Ross only eighty miles north of San Francisco, was still aggressively pursuing trade with native people all along the northwestern Pacific coast.

The army hoped that a show of strength would forestall the necessity to prove it, and its strategy was one of intimidation. On Alcatraz, cannons would occupy the most conspicuous place in the bay, and under ideal conditions, lookouts could scan the entrance to the bay from the island's crest and fire upon invading ships. The military planners were apparently unaware, however, that the bay was, as often as not, shrouded in dense fog. Compounding this problem was the fact that cannons of the period had difficulty hitting even stationary targets at the range of the route past Alcatraz. Ultimately, the chief advantage of the island was its forbidding aura.

Not long after America annexed California, gold was discovered in the foothills of the Sierra Nevada; riches flowed down the rivers from the interior and eddied on the shores of San Francisco Bay. The quiet bay-shore towns there were transformed into commercial carnivals. During the mid-nineteenth century, fortunes were made and lost overnight as characters from all points of origin converged on the Barbary Coast and the population leapt from one thousand to thirty-five thousand during the Gold Rush.

Suddenly, the military's expensive dreams for protection of San Francisco's harbor became urgent necessities. The government poured millions of dollars into the fortification of the bay, the funds coming from a succession of appropriations over a six-year period. In 1853, the government began by building a lighthouse on the island, the first installation of its kind on the West Coast. Among other things, its function was to warn ships away from the dangerous cliffs of Alcatraz.

The army's objective was to make the island even more forbidding in approach, in appearance, in spirit. A dock was constructed in the only possible location, on the east side away from the Pacific Ocean. Blasting and hammering the solid rock, workers then created a ring of platforms for heavy cannon around the island, and a road to connect them. Attackers could only reach this road by passing through a brick sallyport, a deadly corridor designed to funnel the enemy into a chamber where they could be shot at virtually point-blank range. A three-story defensive barracks, or citadel, was dug into the crest of the island. These buildings were of stone, brick, and mortar, their heavy doors of wood strapped and studded with iron. A parade ground for the interminable drilling of the infantry was chiseled into the island.

Eighty-six men garrisoned the fortress of Alcatraz at the end of 1859, to the accompaniment of great fanfare from the press. Alcatraz was now a battle station a third of a mile long, a solid, monumental symbol announcing United States authority from sea to faraway, shining sea. The men stationed on Alcatraz pulled tough duty. They drilled monotonously in the chill, silvery light of the parade ground. They practiced over and over the routine of loading huge cannon—the heavy, clammy iron bruising their numb hands—and waited for their tours of duty to end.

Wearing rough woolen uniforms, marching to and fro to bellowed commands, living in dank, brick barracks, and subsisting on soggy food and stale water . . . this was perhaps not, in itself, so different from many army posts of the time. The difference lay in being on the rock, within sight and even sound of the rollicking city of San Francisco. These soldiers were the straitened drones of a distant federal power, marooned within view of the very center of pleasure, excitement, and sudden fortune.

Alcatraz was naturally suited for confinement, and in 1861, the army transferred thirteen military convicts there from the overcrowded *Presidio* guardhouse. That year, Alcatraz was designated as "Military Prison for the Department of the Pacific," the army's first long-term penal facility. (Previously, soldiers who had been given long jail sentences were sent to civilian prisons.)

Over the next four years, the number of prisoners on Alcatraz increased to about fifty. The army locked up its misfits—brawlers, drunkards, and deserters—and also "enemies" of the United States. When the country burst apart during Civil War (1861-65), emotions were volatile even in California, twenty-five hundred miles away from the battlefields. California was officially allied with the Union cause, but some of its citizens were vocal in their support of the secessionists. *Habeas corpus* had been suspended, and their words, and in a few cases, their actions, landed Southern sympathizers in the guardhouse on Alcatraz.

Californians, who prided themselves on independence and stamina, had taken great risks and worked hard to create new lives, ones that were free of the restrictions of the eastern establishment. California represented the resurrection of personal freedom and opportunity in America, which some felt the industrial Northeast had betrayed. To be locked up in a cold fort without due process of law for speaking one's mind was a bitter outrage. Thus, less than ten years after man first made his mark on it, Alcatraz was already laden with the darker human feelings: anger, defiance, frustration.

Depending upon their status, prisoners sweated out their time shackled to a twelve-pound ball and chain, smashing rocks with sledgehammers, and staggering under the heavy loads of unmechanized construction projects, both on the island and in work parties ashore. By contrast, the authorities of nineteenth-century civilian prisons were experimenting with the concept of rehabilitation through training rather than punishment. Under the predominant Auburn and Pennsylvania systems, most inmates of civilian prisons lived under a rule of silence, walked in lockstep, and were permitted only censored correspondence. They were compelled to participate in vocational training to learn useful trades. Measures were designed to promote the reformation of convicts by teaching them skills and discipline and by encouraging introspection and remorse. Ironically, this made for conditions more irksome to rebellious spirits, even though the guiding philosophy intended to be more humane.

While not at work, Alcatraz prisoners were allowed to go anywhere on the island except the guards' quarters. They could congregate and talk as they wished. Surveillance and routine were less intense, more-or-less limited to the sleeping schedule, group meals, and work assignments. The island was patrolled by guards, often the very men with whom many of the army prisoners had served. There were a number of attempted, and it must be admitted, a few successful escapes. The men who served their time on Alcatraz modified their behavior only to avoid future run-ins with authority, not because they had learned to understand and appreciate the law.

THE ISLAND CONTINUED TO CHANGE under the hand of man. As the technology of war evolved, so did the fortifications on Alcatraz. Huge loads of soil were shipped there to absorb the anticipated blows of incoming shells, should the fortress be attacked. These earthen ramparts gentled the harsh angles of the gouged and scarred rock. Seeds inadvertently brought in with the dirt sprouted, and soldiers planted trees and gardens. Alcatraz nurtured a little greenery for the first time, and provided a habitat for a few more species of birds, insects, and rodents.

The improvements of the 1870s were to be the last effort made by the military to pass Alcatraz off as a strategic post. The original justification for the emplacement of powerful cannons on the island had been "to prevent the passage of hostile vessels" through the Golden Gate. These cannons were never fired in anger, and a notorious incident in 1876 exposed the charade that had been performed through the Civil War and the ensuing decade.

In a mock battle to celebrate the centennial of American independence, the guns of Alcatraz and her sister fortresses on either side of the bay were unable to hit an anchored target ship packed with explosives, in spite of repeated attempts. The people of San Francisco had entrusted their defense to a fortress that was so positioned as to be impotent in the fog, the dark, or even on a clear afternoon. Once again, Alcatraz's justification as defense proved to be an illusion.

The number of cannons on Alcatraz steadily declined through the end of the century, but the island's usefulness did not. The sallyport was enclosed by a large guardhouse to accommodate an increasing population of prisoners.

THE FINAL THIRD OF THE NINETEENTH CENTURY was the great age of American expansion. With the aid of the Homestead Act of 1862, a U.S. Cavalry largely composed of battle-trained Civil War veterans, and the invention of barbed wire in 1874, the West was conquered. The wide-open spaces were fenced for ranches, and plows, mechanical reapers, and threshing machines established productive farms to feed a growing nation. (The population of the United States grew from thirty-one million in 1860 to seventy-six million in 1900.)

The victims of this exuberant expansion were, of course, the Native Americans. Some tried to coexist with white settlers, some fought from the very first contact, but all lost in the end. Many were imprisoned by the army on Alcatraz. Some of the Indians were from "wild," warlike tribes, but even a group of the Hopi ("peaceful") people were shipped to Alcatraz. The Hopi came from thousand-year-old cities in northern Arizona. Deeply religious, their lives on the sunny mesa tops were ordered by the daily prayers of the village crier, cycles of farming, and close clanships. In 1895, a group of Hopi men from Oraibi who opposed allotment of clan-held land to individuals found themselves shipped out to the dim, cold island, where they lived under the glare of armed guards.

All of the Native Americans were imprisoned far from the homes they had fought to save. They could not see their wives or children, nor their aging parents. Entombed on the damp, dead rock, watched over by their enemies, they spent their days tortured by thoughts of what was happening in their absence, longing for and fearing release, drowning in despair.

Deserters, thieves, violent misfits, unrepentant Southern loyalists, and survivors of a spirited but vanquished people—all left Alcatraz with blighted memories and hardened hearts.

During the Spanish–American War and the Philippine insurrection, the use of the island as a strategic point was forgotten. The expansion of the army meant more military prisoners for the island. A temporary stockade was built on the parade ground so that Alcatraz could hold four hundred forty prisoners, more than a tenfold increase over two years. In 1906, during the aftermath of the earthquake, San Francisco was nearly consumed by fire, and the military inmates of Alcatraz were joined briefly by civilian prisoners from the burning city. The prison, like many other structures built on bedrock, was not damaged by the earthquake.

The men housed in the old guardhouse and the temporary stockade on the parade ground were set to work building a new prison in 1908. They tore down the 1858 defensive barracks on the top of the island, leaving only the first floor, which had been dug into bedrock. Beneath the cellhouse they finished in 1912 lies buried a black warren of brick corridors, arches, and studded wooden doors. Cisterns burrowed into the rock still drop into darkness.

The features of the new cellhouse remained essentially the same for the next fifty years; individual cells were arranged in rows. There was a dining hall and hospital. A new generating plant provided electricity. Army prisoners of the twentieth century were the usual outlaws from the enlisted ranks, and more mavericks from the conventional code of patriotism. Conscientious objectors to military service during World War I were jailed there, and a 1918 law making criticism of the government a seditious act provided even more inmates.

Alcatraz was an expensive prison to operate. Everything

had to be shipped from the mainland, including the water used to run the laundry and the fuel to heat it. In addition, a military prison on Alcatraz was an embarrassment: the most conspicuous feature in San Francisco Bay was a jail for bad soldiers. This did nothing for army morale, image, or recruitment. In 1933, the army decided to close the prison.

THE ERA FOR WHICH ALCATRAZ IS MOST FAMOUS then began. The prison became legendary, notorious as the end-of-the-line for America's most diabolical, yet fascinating, characters. Ours is a young country. In our frame of reference, Alcatraz has epic stature. As a federal penitentiary, it held fewer than two thousand prisoners over a mere twenty-nine years. Yet, almost every American knows about it and can even tell a story or two—usually about the "Birdman" or Al Capone.

The Federal Bureau of Investigation was created in 1924 to combat an epidemic of lawlessness that was only just beginning. The Eighteenth Amendment of 1919 (Prohibition) made the manufacture, transportation, or sale of liquor illegal throughout the United States and inadvertently created the bootlegging industry. Illicit distilleries, smuggling, and speakeasies were practically commonplace. The government spent ten million dollars and arrested fifty thousand people annually but could not stop the traffic in alcohol. Before long, gangs managed every aspect of bootlegging, and then rapidly moved into collateral criminal arenas: "protection" rackets, prostitution, robbery, and murder. Exacerbating these problems was the fact that by 1920, there were over seven million automobiles on the road, and criminals were suddenly beyond the reach of local and state authorities. Desperados could rob a bank in one state and slip across to the next in inconspicuous black sedans. Bank robbery, interstate transportation of stolen goods, and—in the wake of the ghastly Lindbergh baby abduction—kidnapping became federal crimes, and the FBI was the nation's police force.

As the crime wave swelled, so did the number of people in prison. In 1925, there were ninety-three thousand in American prisons, or eighty-eight per hundred thousand of population; in 1930, one hundred forty-eight thousand were in jail (one hundred twenty-one per hundred thousand). By 1940, the figure would be one hundred seventy-four thousand prison inmates, or one hundred thirty-two for every hundred thousand American citizens. Yet, with the help of tabloids and Hollywood, gangsters made jokes of federal authority. Partially in response to the social upheaval of the Depression, the gangsters' exploits enthralled America—here were men who scoffed at the law and lived extravagantly and dangerously, men who grew ostentatiously wealthy with the help of corrupt or cowardly public officials. Laborers tied to dreary jobs, or those left jobless by the downward spiral of the economy, followed in fantasy the seemingly glamorous lives of underworld figures.

J. Edgar Hoover, Director of the FBI, was determined to engage these criminals in unrestrained combat. Conservative to an extreme in his private life, Hoover resented the splashy, swaggering style of the gangsters. When Alcatraz Prison became available, Hoover, together with the recently created Bureau of Prisons, set out to make it a place of confinement that would teach a moral lesson not only to its inmates but to the country. Alcatraz was intended to sensationalize the degrading consequences of breaking the law, to rob the underworld of its glamor and appeal. It was to be the maximum penalty short of execution for the most predatory and persistent of criminals.

What was it really like to be imprisoned there? Most U.S. prisons of the 1930s and 1940s were influenced by a reform movement, but Alcatraz was to be a step backward to the rule of silence and absolute control. The men to be confined there were to be deprived of every shred of liberty in every sense of the word and in every detail. The press was seldom allowed on the island and certainly never given the run of it. Allegations were sometimes made by inmates on trial for crimes committed while in Alcatraz—they claimed that men were beaten and left shackled in the dark to the walls of the buried citadel, without food or water.

These accusations were never proven and were waved aside by the men eventually released from Alcatraz; the average stay was eight years, although Alvin "Creepy" Karpis was there for twenty-seven years and nine months for robbing a bank and threatening to "get" J. Edgar Hoover. They said that the ordeals of this most intolerable of prisons were not the obvious ones of physical mistreatment. They were the grimness of regimentation, monotony, complete loss of self. Every day was like every other. The mind and spirit were oppressed by boredom and hopelessness.

Most of the criminals imprisoned on Alcatraz were men who had spent their lives flouting authority. They were accustomed to being in control, to intimidating or eliminating anyone who tried to stand in their way. Suddenly, they had no power at all, and were reduced to the most austere and anonymous level of existence imaginable. A few had led more conventional lives, up to a point. Morton Sobel, convicted of selling secrets to the USSR, had been a mild-mannered, rather intellectual engineer. Protesting his innocence, he had been sent to Alcatraz by Hoover, who abhorred communism and tried to ferret it out with an almost missionary zeal.

What about Robert Stroud, the "Birdman" romanticized by Hollywood as a gentle American Daedelus, a genius who learned the secrets of birds . . . how did he come to be locked up for life? From the *Daily Alaska Dispatch*, (Juneau, Alaska), Tuesday, January 19, 1909:

> F.K.F. VON DAHMER KILLED IN A QUARREL
> Last night between 6:30 and 7 o'clock, F.K.F. Von Dahmer, a bartender employed at the Montana Bar, was shot to death in his cottage on Fourth Street, between Franklin and Gold, by B.F. Straud [sic], a man who recently arrived in this city from Cordova. Two shots were fired by Straud from a .38 calibre Colts revolver, one striking his victim in the temple, while the other struck the wall of the room in which the tragedy occurred. Immediately after firing the fatal shot, Straud walked down Franklin Street, and shortly after gave himself up to City Marshal Mulcahy, who promptly took the prisoner to the Federal jail, where he is now confined . . .
>
> When arrested Straud had no arms on his person, and inquiry revealed that he had left his revolver in the room of a woman known as Kitty O'Brien . . .

> Inquiry this morning developed the following facts: On Sunday evening, Straud, the woman and Von Dahmer were in the house where the killing took place, drinking. Von Dahmer came downtown and told several at the Montana Bar that he had company at his house. It is presumed that Straud became jealous of his attentions to the woman and went to the house last night to settle the grievance, which resulted in the killing . . .

Stroud was sentenced to seven years in prison. Because the murder had been committed in the federal territory of Alaska, he was sent to the federal penitentiary at McNeil Island in Washington state. He was twenty-three years old at the time.

Seven years later, he was on the verge of release from Leavenworth Prison, where he was completing his sentence. Without warning, Robert Stroud savagely stabbed a guard to death in front of twelve hundred inmates and prison authorities in the dining hall. For this apparently motiveless killing, he was sentenced to hang, but the sentence was commuted to life imprisonment in solitary confinement. A fellow convict at Leavenworth Prison, Morris "Red" Rudensky, described Stroud in an interview as "tall, thin, and as attractive as a barracuda or a herring bone without the herring. He seldom spoke to anyone, including the cons, and vice versa. He was a ferocious misanthrope."

Stroud apparently preferred the company of canaries to the conversation of such people. It was at Leavenworth that he carried out his famous research. The authorities permitted him two cells with the intervening wall knocked out in which to keep his birds. He was eventually transferred to Alcatraz, where no such privileges were allowed. He died in prison in 1963, after fifty-four years behind bars.

But for all of them, it was the same. Always the same sights—of one another and the cellhouse. The corridors were always lit. There was no privacy, instead, the continual invasion of strip searches, suspicion, and routine. There was no place an inmate could simply shut the door; toilets were in the open and the men took showers in a bare concrete trough in the basement. Mail and even books and magazines were censored. The isolation cells—pitch black and minimally furnished—offered prisoners the only involuntary privacy they were allowed.

Parallel to the regimentation imposed by authority was the conformity demanded of one another by the inmates. Rival subcultures, complete with hierarchies and arcane jargon, left no one in peace. Independence and character had no chance for expression. As Oscar Wilde put it in *The Ballad of Reading Gaol,* "The vilest deeds like poison weeds bloom well in prison-air: It is only what is good in Man that wastes and withers there . . ."

During the early years, the old-fashioned rule of silence prevailed. Men were not permitted to speak. One can hardly imagine the effusive Al Capone submitting to such a regulation, but he did. They all did. Yet the prison was never quiet. Cell doors clanged, echoing that first time they slammed at one's back. Footsteps of patrolling guards, the grunts and mutterings of other prisoners, and perpetual kitchen clatter raised cacophony within the cellhouse. Booming foghorns, screeching gulls, and the howl of the wind pressed in from outside. (In the later years, inmates could shut out the racket by wearing radio headphones, tuned to programming chosen by the guards.)

The smell of food cooking and of disinfectants liberally sluiced over everything permeated the air indoors. Outside in the exercise yard, there was always the briny tang of the sea and occasionally, a whiff of roasting coffee or chocolate from the processing plants on the mainland. But solid, high walls blocked the view of sea and city. Only those incarcerated in the upper west tier of cells could see San Francisco and the Golden Gate, both far out of reach.

These tough, recalcitrant hoodlums softened and dulled. Steam heat kept the cellhouse stuffy and overwarm. Guards controlled the temperature of the showers, ensuring that they were warm. Food was good, and was served in generous quantities. The exercise yard was no match for this routine and most prisoners became sluggish, then submissive.

Prisoners could receive only infrequent visits from their wives and a few other adults. They were not permitted to see their minor children at all. Both incoming and outgoing mail was censored, purged of all but the most banal content, then recopied by the censors to prevent the sending of secret messages in the paper or penmanship. These men were denied even the pleasure of seeing the handwriting of their loved ones.

Movies provided some relief, but led to expectations the real world could not meet. One inmate wrote in his memoirs that he was shocked at how homely he found most women to be after seeing Hollywood actresses on film for so many years. Chapel was held in Alcatraz; some inmates, listening to the half-forgotten, or perhaps never-before-heard, admonishments, became religious. It is said that George "Machinegun" Kelly served as altarboy while doing time for bank robbery.

Many men spent hundreds of hours researching law, searching for appeal justifications. Others just wanted to serve their sentence and get out. They all tried to maintain some individuality—rearranging the few items in their cells, creating artwork, following exercise routines, maintaining a sense of humor. Trying defiance, malingering, withdrawal. But gradually becoming paler, fatter, more bored and apathetic. A handful were driven to suicide.

Fewer than forty men are known to have tried to escape. They had the time and motivation to spot any flaw, however minute, in the security of the prison. Ten were killed attempting their breaks, another two dozen were recaptured. Officials asserted that the remaining few must surely have perished in the swift, icy waters of the bay.

Those shuffling men . . . had they ever imagined such consequences for their daring escapades? The routine indignities—mass showers, body searches, heavy food at every clockwork mealtime—tantalizing glimpses of the outside world they had never respected—this was their life. They were allowed nothing of their former selves, and for such strong personalities, this must have been worse than flogging.

The government chose to abandon Alcatraz Prison in 1963. It was expensive to operate, and renovations necessary to meet new health and safety regulations would have cost millions of dollars. Criminologists had come to doubt the effectiveness of such a symbol as a deterrent to crime. In August, Attorney General Robert Kennedy ordered the remaining twenty-seven inmates transferred and the prison shut down.

Alcatraz once again became home only to birds and intertidal life. Then in 1969, a group of Native American activists took possession of the island. They lived there for nineteen months, petitioning the government for possession. They knew the bitter history of the place but believed Alcatraz could come to represent the better side of humankind. They hoped to replace the prison with a Native American cultural center, and spent months in discussion and ceremony. Peter Blue Cloud wrote: ". . . her elder children came to purify her desecrated body and to relieve and release the tortured ghosts that suffered there."

Echoing the history of Native American land claims, a federal court ruled their occupation to be illegal. Before they left, some members of the group (which by then included many non-Native Americans) burned and tore down barehanded what they could of the prison that they regarded as a cultural abomination.

STUDIES COMMISSIONED BY THE GOVERNMENT revealed that, incredibly, the American people wanted to visit Alcatraz. Congress passed legislation in 1972 designating it as a national historic site and now, the National Park Service manages the island as part of the Golden Gate National Recreation Area and interprets its story for the public.

Is it bizarre that Alcatraz has become part of the National Park system? Not really, because its story is an integral part of the fabric of American history—a reminder of Spanish exploration, military occupation, and most of all, incarceration. Visiting Alcatraz reveals the utter degradation of prisons and why, when such penalties are possible, the benefit of any doubt is given the accused in our system of justice.

The human history of the island is brief, but scars from its events are everywhere. Alcatraz, initially intended to protect the country from external enemies, has for the most part separated us from internal ones. Alcatraz Prison is a symbol of the darker side of man. As Jung wrote, a symbol "has a wider 'unconscious' aspect that is never precisely defined or fully explained. . . . As the mind explores the symbol, it is led to ideas that lie beyond the grasp of reason."

ALCATRAZ

△ Fog-shrouded fortification.
▷ Lighthouse towers over the ruins of the warden's house.
Preceding pages: Early-morning fog covers San Francisco Bay and Alcatraz.

▷ Stable through old fort gate (double exposure).

△ Old fort.
▷ View of group entering the fort, taken through a gunsight.
Overleaf: Tour entering old fort.

◁ Entrance to lower level of fort.

▷ Brick tunnel in fort's lower level.

△ Entrance to dungeons.
▷ View from the inside of the dungeons.

△ Chain, old fort.
▷ Target practice range, stables.

SAFETY FIRST

△ Shower-cell window, hospital.
◁ Window, stables.

△ Military jail cell, old fort.
▷ Guardtower outside entrance to dungeon.

▷ View of San Francisco from
the burned-out warden's house.

△ Chapel.
◁ The warden's house.

▷ Storm clearing over San Francisco Bay—
Oakland Bay Bridge in the background.

◁ Stairs leading
from the old fort
to the main cellblock.
▷ Fog blowing
by lighthouse and
warden's house.

▷ Prisoners' entrance to the main cellblock.

◁ Cell-door closing control, main cellblock.
▷ Looking down "Broadway," main cellblock.

▷ Near visitors' entrance, main cellblock.

△ Window, main cellblock.
▷ Bars, main cellblock.

▷ Library, main cellblock.
Overleaf: Kitchen gate,
looking toward dining area,
main cellblock.

10
10
11
11

△ Solitary confinement.
◁ "Stripper" cell, solid steel.

▷ Showers, main cellblock.

△ Reflection of windows, factory.
◁ Looking across from "Park Avenue" to "Broadway," main cellblock.
Overleaf: Hospital room.

◁ Entrance to hospital.
▷ Operating room.

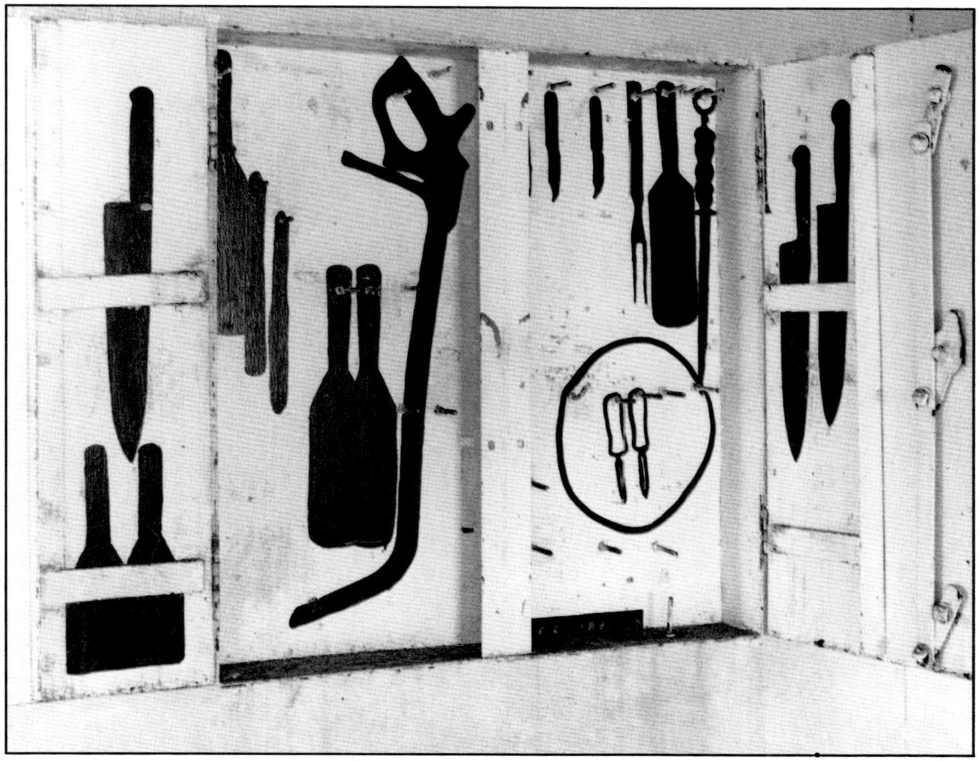

△ Kitchen cabinet.
◁ Outside lock, main cellblock.

Reflections—
warden's house.

◁ Looking toward Pyramid (Transamerica Tower) from factory row.
▷ Factory row.

△ Eagle over entrance to main cellblock.
▷ Stairway housing, main cellblock.

▷ Recreation yard.
Preceding pages: View of
San Francisco skyline
from "Park Avenue,"
main cellblock.

▷ Guard housing level.

△ Flowers outside main cellblock.
◁ Recreation yard.

△ Guardtower.
◁ Guardtower over factory building.
Overleaf: View west toward the Gate.

△ Guardtower, looking west
toward Golden Gate Bridge.
◁ Guardtower, top of "the rock."

Facade, warden's home—
early California architecture.

△ Cormorants.
▷ Entrance to lower level
of main cellblock.

◁ Path to upper level.
▷ Century plants.

△ Watertower.
▷ Wild artichokes.

◁ Century plant, guardtower in background.
▷ Century plant, with main cellblock and lighthouse.

Lighthouse.

◁ View north along factory row, with guards' catwalk.
▷ View along the gardens, toward the Gate (south side).

▷ Sunset over Golden Gate Bridge and Alcatraz.
Preceding pages: Storm clouds over San Francisco skyline.

Designed by David Jenney
Typeset in Bauer Bodoni by Arizona Typographers
Printed by Fabe Litho, Tucson, Arizona
On Simpson Gainsborough and Quintessence Dull
Bound by Roswell Bookbinding, Phoenix, Arizona